How New Life Begins

FOLLETT FAMILY LIFE EDUCATION PROGRAM

How New Life Begins

Esther K. Meeks and Elizabeth Bagwell

Follett Publishing Company   Chicago   New York

Photographic Credits

Cover picture by Russ Kinne, Photo Researchers, Inc.

Alpha Photo Associates, Inc., 22 bottom, 36 lower right; Ron Austing, Photo Researchers, Inc., 6 upper left; Frederick Ayer, Photo Researchers, Inc., 11 right; B. Bhansali from Shostal, 24 right; Black Star, 20 lower left, 24 upper left, 29 left; Ken Brate, Photo Researchers, Inc., 40 lower right; Jane Burton, Photo Researchers, Inc., 21 upper right; Allen Carr, 8 center and upper, middle, and lower right, 9 left and right, 14 lower right, 15 left and upper and lower right, 16 (all four), 17 left, 18 right and middle and lower left, 19 left and lower right, 24 lower left, 26, 44 lower left and right; Cooke, Photo Researchers, Inc., 6 upper right; Ben Dennison, 23 top; Harry Engels, Photo Researchers, Inc., 3; Freelance Photographers Guild, Inc., 2 upper and lower left, upper center and right, 6 lower left and right, 12 upper left, 13 right, 14 upper and middle right, 15 middle right, 20 right, 30 lower right, 34 lower right, 35, 36 left and upper right, 38 upper, middle and lower left, 40 left, 41 upper left; Mario Grassi from Shostal, 18 upper left; Declan Haun, Black Star, 42 top, 46 left, 47 bottom; Inez and George Hollis, Photo Researchers, Inc., 30 upper right; George Holton, Photo Researchers, Inc., 38 right; R. Jaques, Photo Researchers, Inc., 30 left; R. Kinne, Photo Researchers, Inc., 19 upper right, 37; Wallace Kirkland, 20 upper left, 22 top; Jane Latta, Photo Researchers, Inc., 14 upper left; Norman R. Lightfoot, Photo Researchers, Inc., 21 lower right; Christina Loke, Photo Researchers, Inc., 10 upper left; Jesse Lunger, Photo Researchers, Inc., 14 middle left; Michael Mauney, Black Star, 42 lower left and right, 43 (all three), 45, 46 right, 47 top; Tom McHugh, Photo Researchers Inc., 12 lower left; I. A. Mehar from Shostal, 34 left; Hugh Morton from Shostal, 12 right; L. B. Nicholson, Jr., from Shostal, 41 right; Irvin L. Oakes, Photo Researchers, Inc., 8 left, 21 lower left; Dick Robinson, Photo Researchers, Inc., 13 left; B. Rubel from Shostal, 17 lower right; Shostal, 17 upper right, 23 bottom, 31, 39; Ruth H. Smiley, Photo Researchers, Inc., 27; S. Teicher from Shostal, 44 upper left; A. C. Twomey, Photo Researchers, Inc., 10 lower left and right, 11 left; A, Upitis from Shostal, 25, 44 middle left; Joyce R. Wilson, Photo Researchers, Inc., 7; J. D. Winbray from Shostal, 44 upper right; W. H. D. Wince, Photo Researchers, Inc., 14 lower left

Illustrations by Tak Murakami

Designed by Chestnut House

Standard Book Number 695-83855-5 Trade Binding
Standard Book Number 695-43855-7 Library Binding
Standard Book Number 695-23855-8 Educational Binding

Library of Congress Catalog Card Number: 69-13381

Second Printing J

Consultants

John G. Chaltas
Associate Professor of Education
University of New Hampshire
formerly Director of Instruction
Glencoe, Illinois Public Schools

Tess Cogen
Family Life Educator
formerly Director, Family Life Education
The Association for Family Living

Willard Z. Kerman, M.D.
Pediatrician
Past Member and President
Glencoe, Illinois Board of Education

Curtis C. Melnick
Associate Superintendent
Chicago Public Schools

Edward Victor
Professor of Science Education
Northwestern University

Owlets

Pony foal

Moose calf

Baby rabbit and duckling

Young tree seedling

All over the world, new life is always beginning.

Maple trees grow from seeds like this.

Trees make seeds. Some of the seeds take root and grow, so there will always be more trees on earth.

If there were no seeds, there would be no trees in the world when the old trees died.

Flowering plants make seeds so there will always be new young plants and bright new flowers.

Ostrich and eggs

Birds lay eggs. If they did not, some
spring there would be no bird songs.

There would be no bright-colored birds
making nests.

In time, the old birds would die.
Without eggs, there would be no new
young birds.

All kinds of animals and plants keep on making baby animals and plants year after year.

In time, the babies grow up and have babies of their own.

Jack-in-the-pulpit

Opossums have new baby opossums.
Bears have new baby bears.
Tigers have new baby tigers.

Oak trees make acorns.
The acorns grow into
new oak trees.

Dandelions make seeds.
The seeds grow into new
dandelion plants.

A stone cannot make another stone.

A car cannot make another car.

Stones and cars are not living things.

But plants and animals are living things.

They can make new living things like themselves.

16

Barley stalk

Monkeys with young

This is the most wonderful thing about living things.

They can make new living things like themselves.

Which of these things
can make new living things
like themselves?

Plants grow from seeds of the same kind of plant.

Milkweeds grow from milkweeds.

Sunflowers grow from sunflowers.

A milkweed cannot make a sunflower.

Acorns, the seeds of oak trees, make new oak trees.

The seeds of chestnut trees make new chestnut trees.

An oak tree cannot grow from the seed of a chestnut tree.

Fish lay eggs.
Baby fish come from
fish eggs.
Chickens lay eggs, too.
Baby chicks come from
chicken eggs.
A fish cannot grow from
a chicken egg.

Gull's eggs

Maple seeds

GERRY ATWELL FROM NATIONAL AUDUBON SOCIETY
Goose eggs

Wheat

Every egg must be fertilized before it can make a new animal or plant.

Fertilization means that one tiny cell from the male must join with the female egg. The tiny cell is called a sperm.

Poppy

In many plants, sperm cells are made by the pollen. Pollen grows in special parts of flowers.

Inside each unripened seed is a female egg cell.

A sperm must join with this egg before a tiny new plant can grow inside the seed.

The yolk
is the
real female egg
of the chicken.

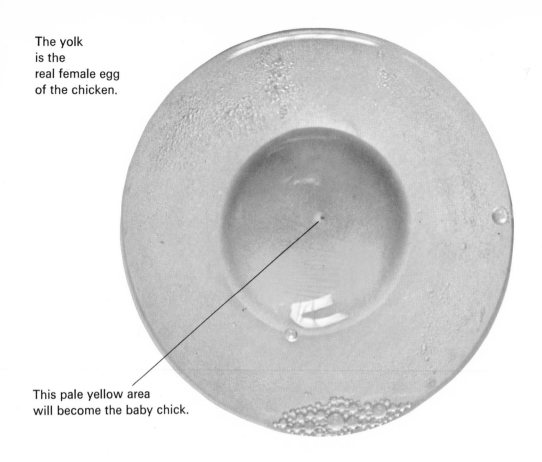

This pale yellow area
will become the baby chick.

In animals, the male cell is also called the sperm cell.

One tiny sperm cell must join with the female's egg before a new animal can begin. This is called fertilization.

The yolk of a chicken's egg is the hen's real female egg.

The part on the yolk that will be a baby chick is very small. The rest is food for the chick until it hatches.

26

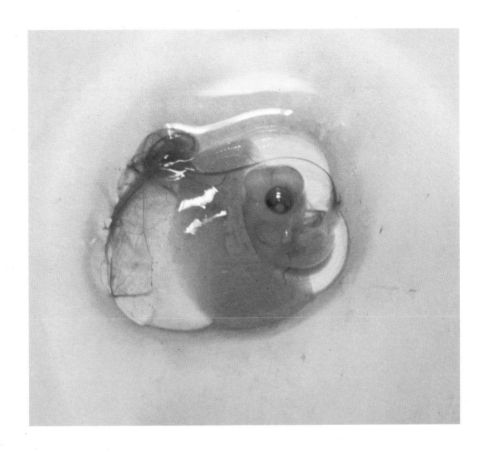

After seven days, the
baby chick inside the egg
looks like this.

The eggs are kept warm
while the baby chick is
growing.

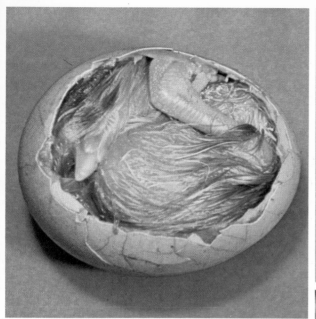

This is how the baby chick looks after three weeks inside the egg.

The food has all been used up.

The chick is ready to live outside the egg shell.

Now it is ready to hatch.

28

Gull's eggs

Turtle

Snake eggs

Other animals lay eggs which can grow into baby animals.

Other birds and many snakes lay eggs. Frogs and toads, fish and turtles lay eggs.

Bison, or buffalo, with calf

Sheep with lamb

Some animals do not lay eggs, but their babies grow from eggs.

These eggs are fertilized by the father's sperm cells while they are inside the mother's body.

Then the babies grow inside the mother until they are ready to live outside.

Goat with kid

30

Horse

The part of the mother's body that the baby grows in is called the uterus.

As the baby grows bigger, the uterus keeps on stretching.

When the baby is ready to be born, the uterus stops stretching.

It slowly begins to squeeze and move the baby down.

The baby is gently squeezed and moved down to an opening between the mother's legs. This is the same opening through which the father's sperm entered the mother's body to join the egg.

Bison or buffalo

Goat

A baby zebra grows inside its mother's body for about twelve months, or one year. Then it is ready to be born and live outside.

Fox pups grow inside their mother's body for almost two months. After that they are ready to live outside.

A calf grows inside the mother cow's body for nine and a half months. Then it is ready to be born.

It takes a baby elephant about twenty-two months, or almost two years, to be ready to be born.

Milk snake

Crocodile

Ducks

Some baby animals can take care of themselves as soon as they are born. They can walk or swim and they can find food for themselves.

36

Turtle

Baboon and baby

Many kinds of animal
babies need help from
their mothers and fathers.

The mothers and fathers
teach the babies how to
find food.

They teach them how to
avoid danger.

Some baby animals grow up very fast.
Deer mice are grown up when they are
about three months old. Then they can
have babies of their own.

Deer are grown up when they are two years old. Then they can have babies of their own.

It takes ten years for a gorilla to grow up.

Human babies take
much longer to grow up
than other babies do.

Mothers and fathers take
care of their boys and girls
for a long time.

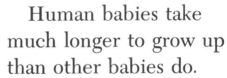

Most boys and girls start
to be grown up when they
are in their early teens.
Their voices change.
Their bodies change.

But it will be several
more years before the boys
and girls are completely
grown up.
Then they will be men
and women.

They will find mates to love. They will marry and have children of their own.

This is the way human life goes on and on.

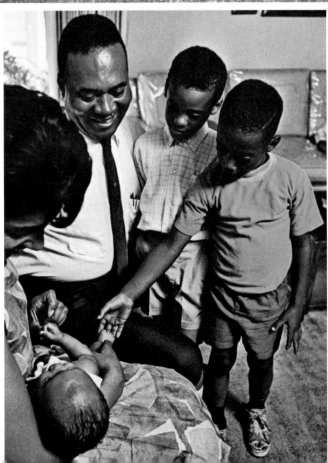